D1305400

WRITING FOR MINECRAFTERS

Grade 1

Sky Pony Press
New York

This book is not authorized or sponsored by Microsoft Corp., Mojang AB, Notch Development AB or Scholastic Inc., or any other person or entity owning or controlling rights in the Minecraft name, trademark, or copyrights.

Copyright © 2019 by Hollan Publishing, Inc.

Minecraft® is a registered trademark of Notch Development AB.

The Minecraft game is copyright © Mojang AB.

This book is not authorized or sponsored by Microsoft Corp., Mojang AB, Notch Development AB or Scholastic Inc., or any other person or entity owning or controlling rights in the Minecraft name, trademark, or copyrights.

All rights reserved. No part of this book may be reproduced in any manner without the express written consent of the publisher, except in the case of brief excerpts in critical reviews or articles. All inquiries should be addressed to Sky Pony Press, 307 West 36th Street, 11th Floor, New York, NY 10018.

Sky Pony Press books may be purchased in bulk at special discounts for sales promotion, corporate gifts, fund-raising, or educational purposes. Special editions can also be created to specifications. For details, contact the Special Sales Department, Sky Pony Press, 307 West 36th Street, 11th Floor, New York, NY 10018 or info@skyhorsepublishing.com.

Sky Pony® is a registered trademark of Skyhorse Publishing, Inc.®, a Delaware corporation.

Visit our website at www.skyponypress.com.

10 9 8 7 6 5 4

Library of Congress Cataloging-in-Publication Data is available on file.

Cover design by Brian Peterson
Cover illustration by Bill Greenhead
Interior illustrations by Amanda Brack and Bill Greenhead
Book design by Kevin Baier

Print ISBN: 978-1-5107-3763-1

Printed in China

A NOTE TO PARENTS

When you want to reinforce classroom skills at home, it's crucial to have kid-friendly learning materials. This *Writing for Minecrafters* workbook transforms writing practice into an irresistible adventure complete with diamond swords, zombies, skeletons, and creepers. That means less arguing over homework and more fun overall.

Writing for Minecrafters is also fully aligned with National Common Core Standards for 1st-grade writing. What does that mean, exactly? All of the writing skills taught in this book correspond to what your child is expected to learn in school. This eliminates confusion and builds confidence for greater homework-time success!

Whether it's the joy of seeing their favorite game characters on every page or the thrill of writing about Steve and Alex, there is something in this workbook to entice even the most reluctant writer.

Happy adventuring!

WRITE WHAT YOU KNOW

Look at the characters below. These characters are also called hostile mobs. Finish the sentence about each hostile mob.

1. The zombie is wearing _____ .

2. The creeper does not have any _____ .

3. The skeleton is tall and _____ .

4. The ghast looks like a _____ .

WRITE YOUR OPINION

Who is the best mob in Minecraft? Finish the paragraph below.

A _____ is the best mob in Minecraft because

_____

_____

_____ .

One example of this is _____

_____

That's why this mob is the best.

MAKE A GUESS

What do you think is happening in the picture? Write your answer below.

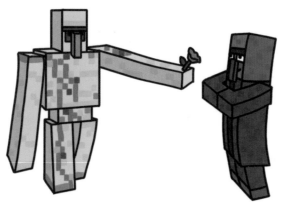

This is an **iron golem**. He guards villages.

This is a **villager**. He lives in the village and he likes to trade.

SILLY FILL-IN

Fill in the words to finish the silly story.

ADJECTIVE
a describing word,
like *scary*

NOUN
a person, place or
thing, like *creeper*

VERB
an action word,
like *run*

One day a baby zombie spawned in _____. He was
_{PLACE}

very _____, so he jumped on a _____ and rode
_{ADJECTIVE} _{ANIMAL}

it to the closest _____ in search of food. When people
_{PLACE}

saw the baby zombie, they began to _____. The baby
_{VERB}

zombie was hungry enough to eat _____ people, but he
_{NUMBER}

didn't want to hurt anyone so he ate a _____ instead.
_{NOUN}

The life of a baby zombie is so _____!
_{ADJECTIVE}

SENTENCE SKILLS

Use the word box to help you write 5 sentences about the picture. Remember to use capital letters at the beginning of each sentence and a period at the end.

barn	butterfly	cat	chickens
pen	fence	pig	sky
horse	red	green.	

1.

2.

3.

4.

5.

PUNCTUATION POWER

These sentences are missing something. Write them correctly on the line below. Every sentence should have a capital letter in the beginning and punctuation (like a period or an exclamation point) at the end.

1. steve is mining for gems

_____

_____

_____

2. steve is using his pickaxe to break the block

_____

_____

_____

3. the block is very hard to break

_____

_____

_____

4. it is good that Steve is so strong

_____

_____

_____

QUOTES

A **quote** is something someone says. A quote begins and ends with a quotation mark. Use the word box to help you finish the quotes.

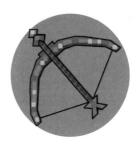

| snowballs | master builder | fast | slow | explode |

1. The creeper said, "I am usually sneaky and quiet. But

_____

sometimes, I _____."

2. "My name is Alex. I am a _____

_____

_____. I love to make things."

3. "Grrrr. Arrgh," said the zombie. "I am very _____,

but dangerous."

4. "I am a wither skeleton. I can run very _____,

so watch out!

5. "I wear a pumpkin as a helmet," said the snow golem. "I

_____

throw _____ at hostile mobs."

SENTENCES

A **sentence** is a group of words that tells a complete thought. All sentences begin with a **capital letter**. A statement ends with a **period**. A sentence includes a **noun**, a **verb**, and sometimes an **adjective**.

ADJECTIVE
a describing word, like *scary*

NOUN
a person, place or thing, like *creeper*

VERB
an action word, like *run*

Read the sentences on the opposite page and follow the instructions below.

1. Draw a triangle around the **capital letter** that begins the sentence.

2. Circle the **noun** (there may be more than one).

3. Underline the **verb**.

4. Draw a rectangle around the **adjective**.

5. Draw a square around the **period** that ends the sentence.

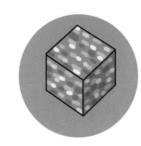

1. The sad skeleton eats ice cream.

2. The chicken lays eggs.

3. The diamond armor is the strongest.

4. The blaze lives in the Nether.

5.  The zombie falls into a lava pit.

NOUNS IN THE NETHER!

*Use the **nouns** in the box to complete the sentences about the Nether. Remember, **nouns** can be a person, a place, or a thing.*

lava	Endermen	Steve	bow	compass

1. _____ spawn in the Nether.

2. The Nether is hot and filled with _____ .

3. A _____ does not work in the Nether.

4. A skeleton spawns with a _____ in its hand.

5. _____ uses a portal to get to the Nether.

VERBS WITH VILLAGERS!

Use the verbs in the box to complete the sentences about villagers. Remember, verbs are action words, like "jump," "make," and "eat."

walk	trade	wears	have	protect

1. The blacksmith _____ black clothing.

2. Villager farmers _____ apples.

3. Iron golems _____ villagers.

4. The zombie villagers _____ slowly.

5. Village libraries _____ seven bookshelves.

MINING FOR ADJECTIVES

*Use the **adjectives** in the box to complete the sentences about Minecraft. Remember, **adjectives** are describing words, like "funny" and "red."*

wooden	hostile	gray	white	loud

1. Steve travels in a _____ minecart.

2. TNT makes a _____ noise when it explodes.

3. The _____ axe can be used to chop wood and other blocks.

4. The mooshroom has _____ spots.

5. The guardian is a _____ mob.

RAINBOWS OF POTIONS!

Potions give you special powers. Each color potion does something different. Write the correct color in the sentences below.

1. _____ potions make you strong.

2. _____ potions shield you from fire.

3. _____ potions are health boosters.

4. _____ potions help you jump higher.

5. _____ potions give you night vision.

6. _____ potions bring you back to health.

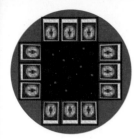

ENDING SENTENCES

Finish the sentences about the End with one of the words in the boxes. The words are a mix of nouns, adjectives, and verbs.

glide	yell	eat

1. Elytra help you _____ .

green	purple	white

2. The end crystal is _____ .

closed	open	broken

3. The ender chest is _____ .

boat	city	shell

4. The shulker hides in its purple _____ .

villager	mob	egg

5. The ender dragon is a boss _____ .

Rewrite the sentences from the previous page on the lines below.

1.

2.

3.

4.

5.

SCRAMBLED!

Use the word box to help you unscramble the words.

bat	firework	ghast
squid	book	melon

1. qidsu

2. tba

3. iefwkorr

4. taghs

5. lomne

6. kboo

torch	witch	ocelot	flower
shulker	arrow	mushroom	

7. letooc _____

8. rorwa _____

9. sumhmoor _____

10. keusrlh _____

11. orhct _____

12. worefl _____

13. iwhct _____

RHYME TIME

Rhyming words are words that sound a lot alike. The words in the boxes rhyme with a word in each sentence. Write the correct rhyming words to complete each sentence.

pig	flowers	sheep	ghast	fish

1. It was a blast hanging out with a _____ .

2. I really wish Steve caught a _____ .

3. The _____ have special powers.

4. A Minecraft _____ cannot dig.

5. The _____ didn't make a peep.

Rewrite the sentences from the previous page on the lines below.

1.

2.

3.

4.

5.

DESCRIBE IT!

Write a sentence next to each picture. Describe what you think is happening in the picture. Remember to use capital letters at the beginning of each sentence and a period at the end.

1.

2.

3.

4.

5.

FINDING FAVORITES

Which picture from the last page is your favorite? Write three sentences about why you like that picture. **Hint: Is it funny? Is it colorful? Does it remind you of something? Explain why you like it the most.**

My favorite picture is

_____

Draw your own version of the picture!

PRONOUN PARTY!

A pronoun is a word that takes the place of a noun. Write the pronouns below.

She	He	It	They

1.

2.

3.

4.

Write the correct pronouns in the spaces below to finish the sentences. If the pronoun comes at the beginning of a sentence, it should start with a capital letter.

1. The shulker spawn egg is purple.

_____ has black spots.

2. Alex is a good builder.

_____ is also a good explorer.

3. The creepers are exploding!

_____ are hostile mobs.

4. Steve had a bad day.

_____ is worried about hostile mobs.

25

VERB PUZZLERS!

There is a lot of action in the game of Minecraft. Verb words are action words. Write 6 sentences using your favorite action words from the box below.

build	farm	walk	spawn	blast
brew	explode	jump	creep	run
craft	fly	mine	grow	

1.

2.

3.

4.

5.

6.

VERB HUNT!

Find the same verbs in the puzzle below and circle them.
Hint: Words can be **diagonal!**

build	farm	walk	spawn	blast
brew	explode	jump	creep	run
craft	fly	mine	grow	

T Z T Y B S C D L Y Q M

T K J Q X U P R G R O W

C B W U E T I A A K U K

R R Q T M X J L W F Q N

E T G F V P P B D N T W

E T W A L K K L B R E W

P B Q R M F L Y O Y K R

X R L M G I N D N D Z V

G T T A Z L N D Y D E D

Z M X Q S Y D E W N N M

J D L R J T T M M Y P T

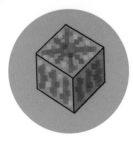

OCELOT IN THE JUNGLE

Imagine what it's like to be an ocelot in the jungle biome. Use the word box to help you write a story of at least 5 sentences about the ocelot. Remember to use capital letters at the beginning of each sentence and a period at the end.

ocelot	biome	parrot	trees
sky	river	drink	monkey

1.

2.

3.

4.

5.

ALEX AND STEVE IN CONVERSATION

Choose the correct words from the word box to fill in the conversation between Alex and Steve.

diamond sword	diamonds	time
cookie	block	creeper

Example:

"Watch out for that _____ **creeper** _____," yelled Alex.

" _____ "

1. Grab your _____ , hollered Steve.

_____ "

2. "Jump over that _____ , she shouted.

_____ "

3. "We need more _____ , yelled Steve.

_____ "

4. "Quick, eat this _____ , I cried.

_____ "

5. "We don't have much _____ , he gasped.

Rewrite the sentences from the last page. Remember that each sentence should start with a capital letter, end with punctuation (like an exclamation mark or a comma), and have quotation marks.

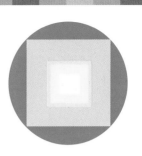

1. _____

2. _____

3. _____

4. _____

5. _____

DEAR JOURNAL

Complete Steve's diary entry below using your imagination and what you know about the game.

Dear diary,

_____

Today I was traveling through the _____

_____

biome and I saw a _____ .

_____

I felt very _____ .

_____

I decided to _____ .

_____

You won't believe what happened next! _____

_____

_____

_____

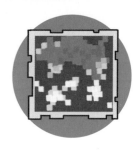

Can you believe what a day I had? I hope tomorrow, I

SILLY FILL-IN

Fill in the words to finish the silly story.

ADJECTIVE
a describing word,
like *silly*

NOUN
a person, place
or thing, like *the
Nether*

VERB
an action word,
like *build*

One night, a family of creepers quietly crept to _____.
                                                    PLACE

The baby creeper made a hissing _____ as they
                                           NOUN

went. Suddenly, a(n) _____ came into sight, and the
                              ANIMAL

_____ creepers all _____. At the same
       ADJECTIVE   VERB, PAST TENSE

time, a bolt of _____ struck and _____
                        NOUN   VERB, PAST TENSE

the baby creeper. The sleeping villagers suddenly _____
                                                         VERB, PAST TENSE

at the sound of the _____. What a _____ night!
                            NOUN   ADJECTIVE

Now, write you own silly story about a spider, a ghast, or another hostile mob. Remember to use capital letters at the beginning of each sentence and a period at the end. Don't be afraid to make it silly!

MINECRAFT MYSTERY

This is **Steve**. Steve is a player in Minecraft. Here he is carrying a diamond sword and wearing a mask.

He is about to do something very sneaky. Write a story about what he is going to do.

WHAT DO YOU SEE?

Look at the illustrations below. Finish the sentence about each illustration. Create your own answers based on what you see.

1. The house is _____.

2. The inside of this chest is _____.

3. The mooshrooms are _____.

4. Steve is holding a _____.

5. The stray zombie is _____.

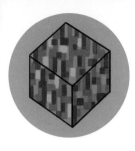

WHAT IN THE WORLD?!

*What is the best **world** in Minecraft? Do you like the Overworld, the Nether, or the End? Finish the paragraph below.*

_____

_____ is the best world in

Minecraft because _____

_____

_____

_____

_____

One example of this is _____

_____

That's why this world is the best.

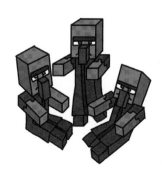

PUNCTUATE IT!

Every sentence should have a capital letter in the beginning and punctuation (like a period) at the end. These sentences are missing something. Write them correctly on the line below.

1. the horse is eating a carrot.

2. The horse has white spots

3. horses eat other vegetables, such as apples

4. The horse is very happy

SIGHT WORDS

Sight words *are some of the words you will see and write most. Write down the sight words you see here!*

where	away	became	please
other	because	which	should
across	together	would	along

1. _____
2. _____
3. _____
4. _____

5. _____
6. _____
7. _____
8. _____

9. _____
10. _____
11. _____
12. _____

Use at least one **sight word** *from this list to write your own sentence about Minecraft.*

_____
_____
_____
_____

Sight words are words you will see and write the most. Write down the sight words you see here!

these	there	them	this
then	they	thank	however
each	caught	sought	brought

1. _____

2. _____

3. _____

4. _____

5. _____

6. _____

7. _____

8. _____

9. _____

10. _____

11. _____

12. _____

*Use at least one **sight word** from this list to write your own sentence about Minecraft.*

_____

_____

_____

_____

BEST OF THE BIOMES

*In your opinion, what is the best **biome** in Minecraft? **Biomes** are areas in Minecraft with different qualities. For example, the desert biome is hot and flat, and the jungle biome has lots of trees and animals. Use the box to choose a biome, and then finish the paragraph below.*

extreme hills	jungle	mushroom islands
savanna	desert	ocean
plains	ice plains	mega taiga
swamp	dark forest	forest

_____

_____ is the best biome in Minecraft

because _____

_____

_____

_____ .

One example of this is _____

_____

_____ .

That's why this biome is the best.

MIX IT UP!

Arrange these mixed-up sentences in the correct order.

1. creeper the exploded green

_____

- -

_____

2. builds Steve bed a

_____

- -

_____

3. dandelion eats a the horse

_____

- -

_____

4. opens Alex an chest enchanted

_____

- -

_____

5. wart nether is a this

_____

- -

_____

SCRAMBLERS

Use the word box to help you unscramble the words.

potion	silverfish	bread
zombie	alex	butterfly

1. vreihsilsf _____

2. ezmobi _____

3. ufybttrle _____

4. xlae _____

5. tioonp _____

6. derab _____

anvil	wither	carrot
blaze	apple	wolf

7. aebzl _____

8. rethiw _____

9. raoctr _____

10. flwo _____

11. valni _____

12. pealp _____

ON THE PLAYGROUND

Use any of the words in the word box to help you write 5 sentences about the picture. Remember to use capital letters at the beginning of each sentence and a period at the end.

chalk	swing	basketball	clouds
red	slide	trees	fence
sky	blue		

1.

2.

3.

4.

5.

WRITING INSTRUCTIONS

*Choose one of the following Minecrafting activities below and write instructions for new players who want to know how to do it. Begin each step with **First, Second, Next,** or **Finally.***

This is how you.... *(Circle one)*

build a bed   tame a wolf

enchant a weapon   make a potion

trade with a villager   battle a _____

---

1. _____

_____

2. _____

_____

_____

3. _____

_____

4. _____

_____

5. _____

DINNER PARTY!

Imagine that you are having a Minecraft mob over for dinner.
Finish the story below.

If I could invite a mob over for dinner, I would invite a _____

_____

_____ .

First I would _____ .

Then I would _____ .

Before he went home, I would _____

_____

_____ .

Having a mob over for dinner would be _____

_____

_____ !

WHAT HAPPENED?

*Change these Minecrafting sentences to the **past tense**. Rewrite each sentence on the lines below to make them **past tense**.*

ran	hid	saw	went	got

1. I **go** to the Nether to fight blazes.

_____

_____

_____

2. I **get** emeralds from a villager.

_____

_____

_____

3. I **hide** from zombies.

_____

_____

_____

4. I **run** to the desert temple.

_____

_____

_____

5. I **see** llamas in the savanna biome.

_____

_____

THE FUTURE IS BRIGHT

*Change this paragraph to the **future tense.** Rewrite the sentences and use the word "will" to make them **future tense.***

1. I go to the End and fight the dragon.

2. I tame a wolf and make it my pet.

3. I build a monster spawner.

4. I brew a potion of underwater breathing.

5. I fight a group of zombies.

SAME AND DIFFERENT

Compare these two hostile mobs. What is the same and different about them? Describe their similarities in the center of the Venn diagram. Describe their differences on the sides.

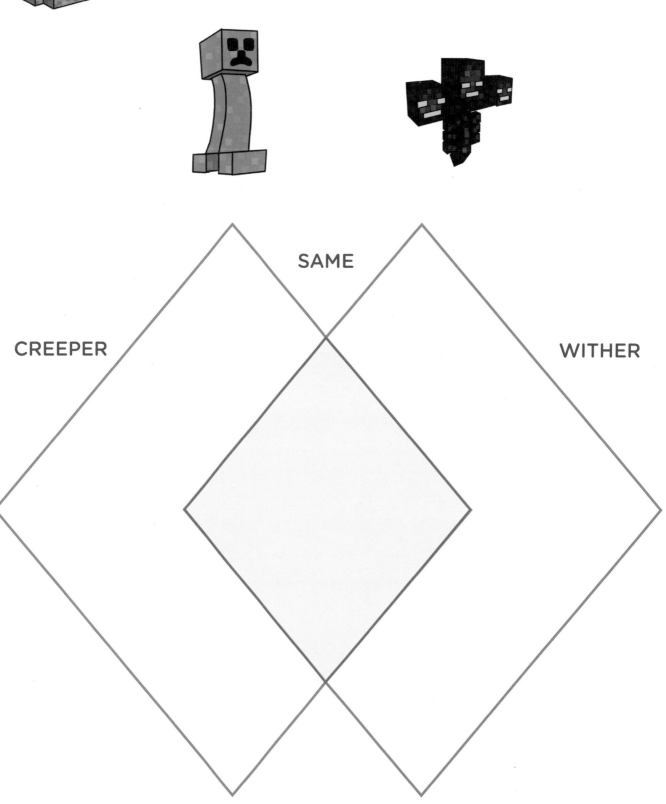

SAME

CREEPER

WITHER

IT'S YOUR ADVENTURE!

Imagine that you have just found elytra in an End city, but you must fight the Ender dragon. Write 5-6 lines about what happens. Choose any of the words in the word box to help you write your story.

dragon	fire	sword	scary
glide	curse	End city	amazing
soar	battle	fall	beast

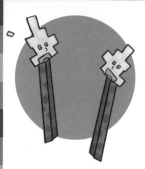

LOST IN A CAVE

Imagine what it's like to be lost in a Minecraft cave. Use any of the words in the word box to help you write a story of at least 5 sentences about how you would get out.

torch	run	walk	jump
mineshaft	minecart	Steve	Alex
creeper	TNT	explode	pickaxe

1. _____

2. _____

3. _____

4. _____

5. _____

YOUR FAVORITE THINGS

Write a few sentences about why you like Minecraft. What makes it fun? How does it make you feel? What is your favorite thing about it?

CERTIFICATE OF ACHIEVEMENT
CONGRATULATIONS

This certifies that

_____

became a

MINECRAFT WRITING BOSS

on _____.
(date)

_____

Signature

ANSWERS

PAGE 8,
PUNCTUATION POWER

1. Steve is mining for gems.
2. Steve is using his pickaxe to break the block.
3. The block is very hard to break.
4. It is good that Steve is so strong.

PAGE 9,
QUOTES

1. "I am usually sneaky and quiet. But sometimes, I **explode**."
2. "My name is Alex. I am a **master builder**. I love to make things."
3. "Grrrr. Arrgh," said the zombie. "I am very **slow**, but dangerous."
4. "I am a wither skeleton. I can run very **fast**, so watch out!"
5. "I wear a pumpkin as a helmet," said the snow golem. "I throw **snowballs** at hostile mobs."

PAGE 11,
SENTENCES

1. The sad skeleton eats ice cream.
2. The chicken lays eggs.
3. The diamond armor is the strongest.
4. The blaze lives in the Nether.
5. The zombie falls into a lava pit.

PAGE 12,
NOUNS IN THE NETHER!

1. **Endermen** spawn in the Nether.
2. The Nether is hot and filled with **lava**.
3. A **compass** does not work in the Nether.
4. A skeleton spawns with a **bow** in its hand.
5. **Steve** uses a portal to get to the Nether.

PAGE 13,
VERBS WITH VILLAGERS!

1. The blacksmith **wears** black clothing.
2. Villager farmers **trade** apples.
3. Iron golems **protect** villagers.
4. The zombie villagers **walk** slowly.
5. Village libraries **have** seven bookshelves.

PAGE 14,
MINING FOR ADJECTIVES

1. Steve travels in a **gray** minecart.
2. TNT makes a **loud** noise when it explodes.
3. The **wooden** axe can be used to chop wood and other blocks.
4. The mooshroom has **white** spots.
5. The guardian is a **hostile** mob.

PAGE 15,
RAINBOWS OF POTIONS!

1. **Red** potions make you strong.
2. **Orange** potions shield you from fire.
3. **Yellow** potion is a health booster.
4. **Green** potion helps you jump higher.
5. **Blue** potion gives you night vision.
6. **Purple** potion brings you back to health.

PAGE 16,
ENDING SENTENCES

1. Elytra help you **glide**.
2. The end crystal is **purple**.
3. The ender chest is **closed**.
4. The shulker hides in its purple **shell**.
5. The ender dragon is a boss **mob**.

PAGES 18 & 19
SCRAMBLED!

1. qidsu **squid**

2. tba **bat**

3. iefwkorr **firework**

4. taghs **ghast**

5. lomne **melon**

6. kboo **book**

7. letooc **ocelot**

8. rorwa **arrow**

9. sumhmoor **mushroom**

10. keusrlh **shulker**

11. orhct **torch**

12. worefl **flower**

13. iwhct **witch**

PAGE 20,
RHYME TIME!

1. It was a blast hanging out with a **ghast**.
2. I really wish Steve caught a **fish**.
3. The **flowers** have special powers.
4. A Minecraft **pig** cannot dig.
5. The **sheep** didn't make a peep.

PAGE 24,
PRONOUN PARTY!

1. **She**
2. **He**
3. **It**
4. **They**

PAGE 25,
PRONOUN PARTY!

1. The shulker spawn egg is purple. **It** has black spots.
2. Alex is good builder. **She** is also a good explorer.
3. The creepers are exploding! **They** are hostile mobs.
4. This is a zombie pigman. **It** spawns when lightning strikes nearby.

PAGE 27,
VERB HUNT!

```
T Z T Y B S C D L Y Q M
T K J Q X U P R G R O W
C B W U E T I A A K U K
R R Q T M X J L W F Q N
E T G F V P P B D N T W
E T W A L K K L B R E W
P B Q R M F L Y O Y K R
X R L M G I N D N D Z V
G T T A Z L N D Y D E D
Z M X Q S Y D E W N N M
J D L R J T T M M Y P T
```

PAGE 30,
ALEX AND STEVE IN CONVERSATION

1. "Grab your diamond sword," hollered Steve.
2. "Jump over that block," she shouted.
3. "We need more diamonds," yelled Steve.
4. "Quick, eat this cookie," I cried.
5. "We don't have much time," he gasped.

PAGE 39,
PUNCTUATE IT!

1. The horse is eating a carrot.
2. The horse has white spots.
3. Horses eat other vegetables, such as apples.
4. The horse is very happy.

PAGE 40,
SIGHT WORDS

1. across
2. along
3. away
4. because
5. became
6. please
7. should
8. together
9. which
10. where
11. would
12. other

PAGE 41,
SIGHT WORDS

1. brought
2. each
3. however
4. other
5. sought
6. thank
7. them
8. then
9. there
10. these
11. they
12. this

PAGE 43,
MIX IT UP!

1. The green creeper exploded.
2. Steve builds a bed.
3. The horse eats a dandelion.
4. Alex opens an enchanted chest.
5. This is a nether wart.

PAGE 44–45,
SCRAMBLERS

1. vreihsilsf silverfish
2. ezmobi zombie
3. ufybttrle butterfly
4. xlae Alex
5. tioonpr potion
6. derab bread
7. aebzl blaze
8. rethiw wither
9. raoctr carrot
10. flwo wolf
11. valni anvil
12. pealp apple

PAGE 50,
WHAT HAPPENED?

1. I **went** to the Nether to fight blazes.
2. I **got** emeralds from a villager.
3. I **hid** from zombies.
4. I **ran** to the desert temple.
5. I **saw** llamas in the savanna biome.

PAGE 51,
THE FUTURE IS BRIGHT

1. I **will** go to the End and fight the dragon.
2. I **will** tame a wolf and make it my pet.
3. I **will** build a monster spawner.
4. I **will** brew a potion of underwater breathing.
5. I **will** fight a group of zombies.